To Emma Jean

From Carol

December 1980

JUST FOR YOU
365 Good Days

The C. R. Gibson Company
Norwalk, Connecticut

*I send you my best wishes
for a year in which you will have
pleasure in living every day
without waiting for the days to be
gone before finding charm in them,
and without putting all hope of pleasure
in the days to come.*

Madame Marie Curie

January 1
The only joy in the world is to begin.

Cesare Pavese

January 2
He is a wise man who does not grieve for the things which he has not, but rejoices for those which he has.

Epictetus

January 3
The art of being wise is the art of knowing what to overlook.

William James

January 4
Prayer does not change God, but changes him who prays.

Sören Kierkegaard

January 5
No one can make you feel inferior without your consent.

Eleanor Roosevelt

January 6
The art of memory is the art of understanding.

Roscoe Pound

January 7
Never grow a wishbone, daughter, where your backbone ought to be.

Clementine Paddleford

January 8
My aim in life has always been to hold my own with whatever's going. Not against: with.

Robert Frost

January 9.
A good listener is not only popular everywhere but after a while he knows something.

Wilson Mizner

January 10
All the great things are simple, and many can be expressed in single words: freedom; justice; honor; duty; mercy; hope.

Winston Churchill

January 11
The first and great commandment is, Don't let them scare you.

Elmer Davis

January 12
The graveyards are full of women whose houses were so spotless you could eat off the floor.

Heloise Cruse

January 13
I like things you don't have to explain because you can't.

Howard Nemerov

January 14
Anyone can do any amount of work, provided it isn't the work he is supposed to be doing at that moment.

Robert Benchley

January 15
There is no opinion so absurd but that some philosopher will express it.

Cicero

January 16
The test of a first-rate intelligence is the ability to hold two opposed ideas in the mind at the same time, and still function.

F. Scott Fitzgerald

January 17
You will do foolish things, but do them with enthusiasm.

Colette

January 18
Friend: one who knows all about you and likes you just the same.

Elbert Hubbard

January 19
No life is so hard that you can't make it easier by the way you take it.

Ellen Glasgow

January 20
What you can become, you are already.

Friedrich Hebbel

January 21
We tire of those pleasures we take, but never of those we give.

Jean Petit-Senn

January 22
I knew nothing better and made the best out of what life offered.
And life is what we make it, always has been, always will be.

Grandma Moses

January 23
My idea of an agreeable person is a person who agrees with me.

Benjamin Disraeli

January 24
The hardest job of all is trying to look busy when you're not.

William Feather

January 25
All that is necessary to make this world a better place to live in is to love—to love as Christ loved, as Buddha loved.

Isadora Duncan

January 26
It has always seemed to me that the best symbol of common sense was a bridge.

Franklin Delano Roosevelt

January 27
Walking isn't a lost art—one must, by some means, get to the garage.

Evan Esar

January 28
Great minds have purposes, others have wishes.

Washington Irving

January 29
Wealth is not his that has it, but his that enjoys it.

Benjamin Franklin

January 30
Man is born broken. He lives by mending. The grace of God is glue.

Eugene O'Neill

January 31
Experience is a hard teacher because she gives the test first, the lesson afterwards.

Vernon Law

February 1
It may be that the race is not always to the swift, not the battle to the strong—but that is the way to bet.

Damon Runyon

February 2
I'm tired of all this nonsense about beauty being only skin-deep. That's deep enough. What do you want—an adorable pancreas?

Jean Kerr

February 3
Work keeps at bay three great evils; boredom, vice, and need.

Voltaire

February 4
Don't part with your illusions. When they are gone you may still exist but you have ceased to live.

Mark Twain

February 5
In the long run you hit only what you aim at. Therefore, though you should fail immediately, you had better aim at something high.

Henry David Thoreau

February 6
It is also said of me that I now and then contradict myself. Yes, I improve wonderfully as time goes on.

George Jean Nathan

February 7
Knowledge begins with wondering. Set a child to wondering and you have put him on the road to understanding.

Samuel Langley

February 8
Nobody ever stubs his toe against a mountain. It's the little temptations that bring a man down.

I.L. Peretz

February 9
Self-pity is our worst enemy and if we yield to it, we can never do anything wise in the world.

Helen Keller

February 10
Few minds wear out; more rust out.

Christian N. Bovee

February 11
Order means light and peace; inward liberty, and free command over one's self; order is power.

Henri Frédéric Amiel

February 12
It is difficult to make a man miserable while he feels that he is worthy of himself and claims kindred to the great God who made him.

Abraham Lincoln

February 13
There are bad people who would be less dangerous if they had no good in them.

François de La Rochefoucauld

February 14
Love is the active concern for the life and the growth of that which we love.

Erich Fromm

February 15
Experience is not what happens to you; it is what you do with what happens to you.

Aldous Huxley

February 16
If you don't get everything you want, think of the things you don't get that you don't want.

Oscar Wilde

February 17
The difference between failure and success is doing a thing nearly right and doing it exactly right.

Edward C. Simmons

February 18
The most serious charge which can be brought against New England is not Puritanism but February.

Joseph Wood Krutch

February 19
Tact consists in knowing how far to go too far.

Jean Cocteau

February 20
The only way to avoid being miserable is not to have enough leisure to wonder whether you are happy or not.

George Bernard Shaw

February 21
The measure of a man's real character is what he would do if he knew he never would be found out.

Thomas Babington Macauley

February 22
I hope I shall always possess firmness and virtue enough to maintain what I consider the most enviable of all titles, the character of an Honest Man.

George Washington

February 23
Most of the trouble in the world is caused by people wanting to be important.

T.S. Eliot

February 24
We should all be concerned about the future because we will have to spend the rest of our lives there.

Charles F. Kettering

February 25
America is a nation with many flaws, but hopes so vast that only the cowardly would refuse to acknowledge them.

James Michener

February 26
A woman's guess is much more accurate than a man's certainty.

Rudyard Kipling

February 27
Peace is art. Peace is when time doesn't matter as it passes by.

Maria Schell

February 28
Conscience is a mother-in-law whose visit never ends.

H. L. Mencken

February 29
A man usually falls in love with the woman who asks the kind of questions he is able to answer.

Ronald Colman

March 1
If I shoot at the sun, I may hit a star.

P. T. Barnum

March 2
Never economize on luxuries.

Angela Thirkell

March 3
None can love freedom heartily but good men; the rest love not freedom but license.

John Milton

March 4
Good to forgive;
Best to forget.

Robert Browning

March 5
Back of tranquility lies always conquered unhappiness.

David Grayson

March 6
So live that your life may be a poem. Arrange things so that they look like they are in a painting.

Chang Chao

March 7
Save a boyfriend for a rainy day—and another, in case it doesn't rain.

Mae West

March 8

In all ranks of life the human heart yearns for the beautiful; and the beautiful things that God makes are his gift to all alike.

Harriet Beecher Stowe

March 9

Winning has always meant much to me, but winning *friends* has meant the most.

Mildred "Babe" Didrikson

March 10

Admiration. Our polite recognition of another's resemblance to ourselves.

Ambrose Bierce

March 11

Earnest people are often people who habitually look on the serious side of things that have no serious side.

Van Wyck Brooks

March 12

One of the best ways to persuade others is with your ears—by listening to them.

Dean Rusk

March 13

He who attracts luck carries with him the magnet of preparation.

William A. Ward

March 14

I've never been poor, only broke. Being poor is a frame of mind. Being broke is only a temporary situation.

Mike Todd

March 15

A man's mind stretched by a new idea can never go back to its original dimensions.

Oliver Wendell Holmes

March 16

Thinking is more interesting than knowing, but less interesting than looking.

Johann von Goethe

March 17
Women like silent men. They think they're listening.

Marcel Achard

March 18
Fortune and Love befriend the bold.

Ovid

March 19
A man who finds no satisfaction in himself, will not find it elsewhere.

François de La Rochefoucauld

March 20
Be humble, for the worst thing in the world is of the same stuff as you; be confident, for the stars are of the same stuff as you.

Nicholai Velimirovic

March 21
Politicians are the same all over. They promise to build a bridge even where there is no river.

Nikita Khrushchev

March 22
Seeing is deceiving. It's eating that's believing.

James Thurber

March 23
We judge ourselves by what we feel capable of doing, while others judge us by what we have already done.

Henry Wadsworth Longfellow

March 24
Wit has truth in it; wisecracking is simply calisthenics with words.

Dorothy Parker

March 25
It is a tolerable depiction of a bore that he is one who talks about himself when you want to talk about yourself.

Robert Hugh Benson

March 26
An artist's career always begins tomorrow.

James McNeill Whistler

March 27
The fact that boys are allowed to exist at all is evidence of a remarkable Christian forbearance among men.

Ambrose Bierce

March 28
It is not true that life is one damn thing after another—it's one damn thing over and over.

Edna St. Vincent Millay

March 29
The age of discretion is reached when one has learned to be indiscreet discreetly.

Tommy Pollard

March 30
Half the modern drugs could well be thrown out the window, except that the birds might eat them.

Martin H. Fischer

March 31
The world is round and the place which may seem like the end may also be only the beginning.

Ivy Baker Priest

April 1
April 1. This is the day upon which we are reminded of what we are on the other three hundred and sixty-four.

Mark Twain

April 2
Never learn to do anything. If you don't learn you'll always find someone else to do it for you.

Mark Twain's Mother

April 3
Women are wiser than men because they know less and understand more.

James Stephens

April 4
The winds and waves are always on the side of the ablest navigators.

Edward Gibbon

April 5

It never occurs to fools that merit and good fortune are closely united.

Johann von Goethe

April 6

People who fly into a rage always make a bad landing.

Will Rogers

April 7

A man should never be ashamed to own he has been in the wrong, which is but saying, in other words, that he is wiser today than he was yesterday.

Alexander Pope

April 8

Great tranquillity of heart is his who cares for neither praise nor blame.

Thomas À Kempis

April 9

Rare is the person who can weigh the faults of others without putting his thumb on the scales.

Byron Langenfeld

April 10

The physician can bury his mistakes, but the architect can only advise his clients to plant vines.

Frank Lloyd Wright

April 11

I am not afraid of tomorrow, for I have seen yesterday and I love today.

William Allen White

April 12

The first and worst of all frauds is to cheat one's self.

Philip James Bailey

April 13

Parents were invented to make children happy by giving them something to ignore.

Ogden Nash

April 14
There are several ways in which to apportion the family income, all of them unsatisfactory.

Robert Benchley

April 15
To produce an income tax return that has any depth to it, any feeling, one must have lived—and suffered.

Frank Sullivan

April 16
If you would know the value of money go and try to borrow some.

Benjamin Franklin

April 17
I believe that what woman resents is not so much giving herself in pieces as giving herself purposelessly.

Anne Morrow Lindbergh

April 18
"Be yourself" is about the worst advice you can give some people.

Tom Masefield

April 19
The flour is the important thing, not the mill; the fruits of philosophy, not the philosophy itself. When we ask what time it is we don't want to know how the watch was constructed.

G. C. Lichtenberg

April 20
The only thing necessary for the triumph of evil is for good men to do nothing.

Edmund Burke

April 21
Life is an unanswered question, but let's still believe in the dignity and importance of the question.

Tennessee Williams

April 22
All that we are is the result of what we have thought. The mind is everything. What we think, we become.

Buddha

April 23

Our national flower is the concrete cloverleaf.

Lewis Mumford

April 24

People don't choose their careers; they are engulfed by them.

John Dos Passos

April 25

Trying to define yourself is like trying to bite your own teeth.

Alan Watts

April 26

In these times you have to be an optimist to open your eyes when you awake in the morning.

Carl Sandburg

April 27

What passes for optimism is most often the effect of an intellectual error.

Raymond Aron

April 28

How glorious it is—and also how painful—to be an exception.

Alfred De Musset

April 29

A bachelor never quite gets over the idea that he is a thing of beauty and a boy forever.

Helen Rowland

April 30

Three be the things I shall have till I die: Laughter and hope and a sock in the eye.

Dorothy Parker

May 1

All mankind love a lover.

Ralph Waldo Emerson

May 2

All the world loves a lover—unless he is in a telephone booth.

Dave Tomick

May 3

Education is the ability to listen to almost anything without losing your temper or your self-confidence.

Robert Frost

May 4

A highbrow is a man who has found something more interesting than women.

Edgar Wallace

May 5

Men have more problems than women. In the first place, they have to put up with women.

Françoise Sagan

May 6

To live is good. To live vividly is better. To live vividly together is best.

Max Eastman

May 7

I have a simple philosophy: Fill what's empty, empty what's full and scratch where it itches.

Alice Roosevelt Longworth

May 8

The great tragedies of history occur not when right confronts wrong, but when two rights confront each other.

Henry A. Kissinger

May 9

He who slings mud generally loses ground.

Adlai Stevenson

May 10

It is very easy to forgive others their mistakes; it takes more grit to forgive them for having witnessed your own.

Jessamyn West

May 11

Civilization is always in danger when those who have never learned to obey are given the right to command.

Fulton J. Sheen

May 12
Too often travel, instead of broadening the mind, merely lengthens the conversation.

Elizabeth Drew

May 13
While the right to talk may be the beginning of freedom, the necessity of listening is what makes that right important.

Walter Lippman

May 14
Middle age: When you're sitting at home on Saturday night and the telephone rings and you hope it isn't for you.

Ogden Nash

May 15
Any girl can be glamorous. All you have to do is stand still and look stupid.

Hedy Lamarr

May 16
Age doesn't matter, unless you're a cheese.

J. Paul Getty

May 17
A woman is as old as she looks to a man that likes to look at her.

Finley Peter Dunne

May 18
In the space age, man will be able to go around the world in two hours—one hour flying and the other to get to the airport.

Neil McElroy

May 19
Inside myself is a place where I live all alone and that's where you renew your springs that never dry up.

Pearl Buck

May 20
My theory is that men are no more liberated than women. I suppose that leadership at one time meant muscle; but today it means getting along with people.

Indira Gandhi

May 21
The most incomprehensible thing about the world is that it is comprehensible.

Albert Einstein

May 22
Some things have to be believed to be seen.

Ralph Hodgson

May 23
Humility is strong—not bold; quiet—not speechless, sure—not arrogant.

Estelle Smith

May 24
I believe in getting into hot water. I think it keeps you clean.

G. K. Chesterton

May 25
The most exhausting thing in life is being insincere.

Anne Morrow Lindbergh

May 26
We have a bat's eyes for our own faults, and an eagle's for the faults of others.

J. L. Gordon

May 27
Character is made by what you stand for, reputation by what you fall for.

Alexander Woollcott

May 28
I have the simplest tastes. I am always satisfied with the best.

Oscar Wilde

May 29
Television: chewing gum for the eyes.

Frank Lloyd Wright

May 30
People will buy anything that's one to a customer.

Sinclair Lewis

May 31

I just want one word on my tombstone: "Even." I was born even, and I want to go out even.

Joe Louis

June 1

A guy who throws what he intends to throw—that's the definition of a good pitcher.

Sandy Koufax

June 2

Money is what you'd get on beautifully without if only other people weren't so crazy about it.

Margaret Case Harriman

June 3

It is hard to imagine a civilization without onions.

Julia Child

June 4

The worst-tempered people I've ever met were people who knew they were wrong.

Wilson Mizner

June 5

He must have had a magnificent build before his stomach went in for a career of its own.

Margaret Halsey

June 6

I like snobs. A snob has to spend so much time being a snob that he has little time left to meddle with you.

William Faulkner

June 7

Things are never quite the same somehow after you have to lie to a person.

Christopher Morley

June 8

Time, whose tooth gnaws away everything else, is powerless against truth.

Thomas H. Huxley

June 9

The trouble with being punctual is that nobody's there to appreciate it.

Franklin P. Jones

June 10

When you say that you agree to a thing in principle, you mean that you have not the slightest intention of carrying it out in practice.

Otto von Bismarck

June 11

Killing time is suicide on the installment plan.

T. E. Burke

June 12

Culture is what your butcher would have if he were a surgeon.

Mary Pettibone Poole

June 13

Beware of all enterprises that require new clothes.

Henry David Thoreau

June 14

Grumbling is the death of love.

Marlene Dietrich

June 15

A speck cuts the value of a diamond in half—a race horse that can run a mile a few seconds faster is worth twice as much. That little extra proves to be the greatest value.

John D. Hess

June 16

Conscience is the perfect interpreter of life.

Karl Barth

June 17

The rush of power to the head is not as becoming as a new hat.

Helen Van Slyke

June 18

One sign of maturity is the ability to be comfortable with people who are not like us.

Virgil A. Kraft

June 19
Faith has to do with the basis, the ground on which we stand. Hope is reaching out for something to come. Love is just being there and acting.

Emil Brunner

June 20
Don't laugh at a youth for his affectations; he is only trying on one face after another to find his own.

Logan Pearsall Smith

June 21
Summer is the season when children slam the doors they left open all winter.

Mary Raynor

June 22
Persons are to be loved; things are to be used.

Reuel Howe

June 23
Big doesn't necessarily mean better. Sunflowers aren't better than violets.

Edna Ferber

June 24
Hatred toward any human being cannot exist in the same heart as love to God.

Dean William Ralph Inge

June 25
I will not permit any man to narrow and degrade my soul by making me hate him.

Booker T. Washington

June 26
You're supposed to think like a man, dress like a queen, speak like a lady and work like a dog.

Eva Adams

June 27
Morality may consist solely in the courage of making a choice.

Leon Blum

June 28
The men who are lifting the world upward and onward are those who encourage more than criticize.

Elisabeth Harrison

June 29
Fanaticism consists in redoubling your efforts when you have forgotten your aim.

George Santayana

June 30
No person was ever honored for what he received; honor has been the reward for what he gave.

Calvin Coolidge

July 1
Man, like the bridge, was designed to carry the load of the moment, not the combined weight of a year at once.

William A. Ward

July 2
We feel free when we escape—even if it be but from the frying pan into the fire.

Eric Hoffer

July 3
The tragedy of life is not so much what men suffer, but rather what they miss.

Thomas Carlyle

July 4
We have inherited the great principles upon which liberty is based, but we have not inherited liberty. That must be secured and maintained by every new generation.

John J. Sirica

July 5
The real rewards that come to you in life are loyalties.

Thomas Hart Benton

July 6
There is one thing about baldness—it's neat.

Don Herold

July 7

Equality is not when a female Einstein gets promoted to assistant professor. Equality is when a female schlemiel moves ahead as fast as a male schlemiel.

Ewald B. Nyquist

July 8

A good scare is worth more to a man than good advice.

Edgar W. Howe

July 9

Passport Photo: If I look like this, I need the trip.

Gloria Swanson

July 10

It is amazing how nice people are to you when they know you are going away.

Michael Arlen

July 11

Democracy is like a raft: It won't sink, but you will always have your feet wet.

Russell B. Long

July 12

I rise from bed the first thing in the morning not because I am dissatisfied with it, but because I cannot carry it with me during the day.

Edgar Wilson Nye

July 13

It hurts more to have a belief pulled than to have a tooth pulled, and no intellectual Novocain is available.

Elmer Davis

July 14

No man likes to have his intelligence or good faith questioned, especially if he has doubts about it himself.

Henry Adams

July 15

Heaven grant us patience with a man in love.

Rudyard Kipling

July 16
When you see a married couple coming down the street, the one
who is two steps ahead is the one that's mad.

Helen Rowland

July 17
There is only one way to achieve happiness on this terrestrial ball,
And that is to have either a clear conscience, or none at all.

Ogden Nash

July 18
Really, I'm a square. But it's the squares who carry the burden of the
world, and the bores who become heroes.

Katharine Hepburn

July 19
There's nothing terrible about being "square." The "squares" are the
ones who make the clothes, bake the bread, build the houses, and
even make the motorcycles.

Bob Hope

July 20
The existence of forgetting has never been proved: we only know
that some things don't come to mind when we want them.

Friedrich Nietzsche

July 21
When you convert someone to an idea . . . you lose your faith in it.

Oscar Wilde

July 22
If you lend a friend five dollars and never see him again, it's worth it.

Martin Gardner

July 23
When two men in business always agree, one of them is
unnecessary.

William Wrigley, Jr.

July 24
I have 13 dependents. All of them have 140 IQ or better, except me.
I'm under 100 and I support them all.

Chi Chi Rodriguez

July 25
Worry is interest paid on trouble before it becomes due.

Dean William Ralph Inge

July 26
Back of every achievement is a proud wife and a surprised mother-in-law.

Brooks Hays

July 27
We can only love what we know and we can never know completely what we do not love.

Aldous Huxley

July 28
Anything you're good at contributes to happiness.

Bertrand Russell

July 29
The thing that impresses me most about America is the way parents obey their children.

Duke of Windsor

July 30
In the final analysis our most basic common link is that we all inhabit this small planet. We all breathe the same air. We all cherish our children's future. And we all are mortal.

John F. Kennedy

July 31
The fundamental defect of fathers is that they want their children to be a credit to them.

Bertrand Russell

August 1
Today one is ashamed of being ashamed of things of which he was ashamed yesterday.

Jacques Tati

August 2
The man who never alters his opinion is like standing water, and breeds reptiles of the mind.

William Blake

August 3
Most people would die sooner than think; in fact, they do so.

Bertrand Russell

August 4
Thinking isn't to agree or disagree. That's voting.

Robert Frost

August 5
Everyone is the age he has decided on, and I have decided to remain 30 years old.

Pablo Picasso

August 6
If my husband would ever meet a woman on the street who looked like the women in his paintings, he would fall over in a dead faint.

Madame Pablo Picasso

August 7
Many a man wishes he were strong enough to tear a telephone book in half—especially if he has a teen-age daughter.

Guy Lombardo

August 8
In heaven when the blessed use the telephone they will say what they have to say and not a word besides.

W. Somerset Maugham

August 9
Could we know what men are most apt to remember, we might know what they are most apt to do.

George Savile

August 10
Never answer a question, other than an offer of marriage, by saying Yes or No.

Susan Chitty

August 11
I admire the serene assurance of those who have religious faith. It is wonderful to observe the calm confidence of a Christian with four aces.

Mark Twain

August 12
In this world, there is always danger for those who are afraid of it.

George Bernard Shaw

August 13
Perhaps host and guest is really the happiest relation for father and son.

Evelyn Waugh

August 14
There is no dignity quite so impressive, and no independence quite so important, as living within your means.

Calvin Coolidge

August 15
The day will happen whether or not you get up.

John Ciardi

August 16
My education was so sound that I know hardly anything.

Ronald MacKenzie

August 17
We have too many people who live without working, and we have altogether too many who work without living.

Charles R. Brown

August 18
I would give up all my fame and all my art if there were one woman who cared whether or not I came home late for dinner.

Ivan Turgenev

August 19
As you grow old you have fewer joys but more interests.

Françoise Sagan

August 20
The public is like a piano. You just have to know what keys to poke.

Al Capp

August 21
He who wants to know people should study their excuses.

Friedrich Hebbel

August 22
A private railroad car is not an acquired taste. One takes to it
immediately.

Mrs. August Belmont

August 23
Husbands are like fires. They go out when unattended.

Zsa Zsa Gabor

August 24
Wisdom consists not so much in knowing what to do in the ultimate
as in knowing what to do next.

Herbert Hoover

August 25
How can you be expected to govern a country that has 246 kinds of
cheese?

Charles de Gaulle

August 26
There is no security on this earth; there is only opportunity.

Douglas MacArthur

August 27
There is luxury in self-reproach . . . when we blame ourselves we feel
no one else has a right to blame us.

Oscar Wilde

August 28
The men who try to do something and fail are infinitely better than
those who try to do nothing and succeed.

Lloyd Jones

August 29
The wisest man I have ever known once said to me: "Nine out of
every ten people improve on acquaintance"; and I have found his
words true.

Frank Swinnerton

August 30
Really great men have a curious feeling that the greatness is not in
them but through them.

John Ruskin

August 31
We can do noble acts without ruling earth and sea.

Aristotle

September 1
Things don't change, but by and by our wishes change.

Marcel Proust

September 2
Despair is the conclusion of fools.

Benjamin Disraeli

September 3
An appeaser is one who feeds a crocodile—hoping it will eat him last.

Winston Churchill

September 4
Hating people is like burning down your own house to get rid of a rat.

Harry Emerson Fosdick

September 5
It is only with the heart that one can see rightly; what is essential is invisible to the eye.

Antoine de Saint-Exupéry

September 6
Being an old maid is like death by drowning, a really delightful sensation after you cease to struggle.

Edna Ferber

September 7
Disappointments are to the soul what a thunder-storm is to the air.

Johann von Schiller

September 8
Without God the world would be a maze without a clue.

Woodrow Wilson

September 9
The penalty of success is to be bored by the people who used to snub you.

Nancy, Lady Astor

September 10
Nobody can describe a fool to the life without much patient self-inspection.

Frank Moore Colby

September 11
I have often thought what a melancholy world this would be without children, and what an inhuman world without the aged.

Samuel Taylor Coleridge

September 12
Caesar might have married Cleopatra, but he had a wife at home. There's always something.

Will Cuppy

September 13
Who rises from prayer a better man, his prayer is answered.

George Meredith

September 14
Our society in America is founded upon a faith in man as an end in itself.

David Lilienthal

September 15
All I can say for the United States Senate is that it opens with a prayer, and closes with an investigation.

Will Rogers

September 16
Many a man that can't direct you to a corner drugstore will get a respectful hearing when age has further impaired his mind.

Finley Peter Dunne

September 17
Drying a widow's tears is one of the most dangerous occupations known to man.

Dorothy Dix

September 18
Hit the ball over the fence and you can take your time going around the bases.

John W. Raper

September 19
As soon as you can't keep anything from a woman, you love her.

Paul Geraldy

September 20
Two can live as cheap as one, but it costs them twice as much.

Frank Sullivan

September 21
Always do one thing less than you think you can do.

Bernard M. Baruch

September 22
He who fears he will suffer, already suffers because of his fear.

Michel de Montaigne

September 23
A farm is an irregular patch of nettles bounded by short-term notes, containing a fool and his wife who didn't know enough to stay in the city.

S. J. Perelman

September 24
Laugh at yourself first, before anyone else can.

Elsa Maxwell

September 25
Thy friend has a friend, and thy friend's friend has a friend. Be discreet.

The Talmud

September 26
You can close your eyes to reality but not to memories.

Stanislaus Lec

September 27
To be brief is almost a condition of being inspired.

George Santayana

September 28
Three-fourths of the people you will meet tomorrow are hungering and thirsting for sympathy. Give it to them, and they will love you.

Dale Carnegie

September 29
The greatest happiness is to be that which one is.

Theodore Herzl

September 30
Never work before breakfast; if you have to work before breakfast, eat your breakfast first.

Josh Billings

October 1
Football makes a nation hardy. You build up a lot of strong resistance sitting on a cold concrete seat.

Herbert V. Prochnow

October 2
An atheist is a guy who watches a Notre Dame-SMU football game and doesn't care who wins.

Dwight D. Eisenhower

October 3
A polite man is one who listens with interest to things he knows about, when they are told to him by a person who knows nothing about them.

Phillipe de Mornay

October 4
He who believes in nobody knows that he himself is not to be trusted.

Berthold Auerbach

October 5
Find out where you can render a service, and then render it. The rest is up to the Lord.

S. S. Kresge

October 6
Never argue at the dinner table, for the one who is not hungry always gets the best of the argument.

Richard Whately

October 7
We think in generalities, but we live in detail.

Alfred North Whitehead

October 8
His passions make man live, his wisdom merely makes him last.

Sebastian Chamfort

October 9
No man who has wrestled with a self-adjusting card table can ever be quite the man he once was.

James Thurber

October 10
It was not guns that broke Napoleon on the Moscow road; it was the might of the snowflakes.

James Reid

October 11
Except when it comes to bravery, we are a nation of mice. We dress and behave with timid circumspection. Good taste is the worst vice ever invented.

Edith Sitwell

October 12
We didn't all come over on the same ship, but we're all in the same boat.

Bernard M. Baruch

October 13
The aim of a college education is to teach you to know a good man when you see one.

William James

October 14
Remember when people worried about how much it took to buy something, instead of how long?

Earl Wilson

October 15
He who praises you for what you lack wishes to take from you what you have.

Juan Manuel

October 16
If at first you don't succeed you're running about average.

M. H. Alderson

October 17
If you watch a game, it's fun. If you play it, it's recreation. If you work at it, it's golf.

Bob Hope

October 18
Tact is the knack of making a point without making an enemy.

Howard W. Newton

October 19
We learn from experience. A man never wakes up his second baby just to see it smile.

Grace Williams

October 20
The only real argument for marriage is that it remains the best method for getting acquainted.

Heywood Broun

October 21
Middle age is when you don't have to have fun to enjoy yourself.

Franklin P. Jones

October 22
I begin to realize that I am growing old: the taxi driver calls me "Pop" instead of "Buddy."

Alexander Woollcott

October 23
Keep what is worth keeping—
And with the breath of kindness
Blow the rest away.

Dinah Maria Mulock Craik

October 24
Kindness is a language the dumb can speak and the deaf can hear and understand.

Christian N. Bovee

October 25
The only real elegance is in the mind; if you've got that, the rest really comes from it.

Diana Vreeland

October 26
Nothing is particularly hard if you divide it into small jobs.

Henry Ford

October 27
People who work sitting down get paid more than people who work standing up.

Ogden Nash

October 28
Life demands from you only the strength you possess. Only one feat is possible—not to have run away.

Dag Hammarskjold

October 29
He who has a claim for money upon his neighbor and knows that he is unable to pay, must not keep crossing his path.

The Talmud

October 30
Any song that moves you to joy or tears has greatness. Everything in life should be enjoyed for what it is.

Marguerite Piazza

October 31
There is nothing final about a mistake, except its being taken as final.

Phyllis Bottome

November 1
Don't be afraid to take a big step if one is indicated. You can't cross a chasm in two small jumps.

David Lloyd George

November 2
I've run more risk eating my way across the country than in all my driving.

Duncan Hines

November 3
In helping others, we shall help ourselves, for whatever good we give out completes the circle and comes back to us.

Flora Edwards

November 4
The sweetest revenge is to forgive.

Isaac Friedmann

November 5
It is the content of our lives that determines their value. If we limit ourselves to supply the means of living, in what way have we placed ourselves above the cattle that graze the fields?

Arthur Holly Compton

November 6
Less is more.

Mies van der Rohe

November 7
No man is lonely while eating spaghetti—it requires so much attention.

Christopher Morley

November 8
It's when you're safe at home that you wish you were having an adventure. When you're having an adventure you wish you were safe at home.

Thornton Wilder

November 9
An artist carries on throughout his life a mysterious, uninterrupted conversation with his public.

Maurice Chevalier

November 10
Everybody has to be somebody to somebody to be anybody.

Malcolm S. Forbes

November 11
You are part of the Infinite. This is your nature. Hence you are your brother's keeper.

Vivekananda

November 12
A play should give you something to think about. When I see a play and understand it the first time, then I know it can't be much good.

T. S. Eliot

November 13
Playing Shakespeare is so tiring. You never get a chance to sit down unless you're a King.

Josephine Hull

November 14
Finance is the art of passing currency from hand to hand until it finally disappears.

Robert W. Sarnoff

November 15
Blessed are those who can give without remembering, and take without forgetting.

Elizabeth Bibesco

November 16
Procrastination is the art of keeping up with yesterday.

Don Marquis

November 17
It is a miserable thing to live in suspense; it is the life of a spider.

Jonathan Swift

November 18
Tired mothers find that spanking takes less time than reasoning and penetrates sooner to the seat of memory.

Will Durant

November 19
When a man seeks your advice he generally wants your praise.

Lord Chesterfield

November 20
It is easier to fight for one's principles than to live up to them.

Alfred Adler

November 21
Art is nothing less than a way of making joys perpetual.

Rebecca West

November 22
Never trust the advice of a man in difficulties.

Aesop

November 23
Be awful nice to 'em goin' up, because you're gonna meet 'em all comin' down.

Jimmy Durante

November 24
Repartee: What a person thinks of after he becomes a departee.

Dan Bennett

November 25
From birth to eighteen, a girl needs good parents. From eighteen to thirty-five, she needs good looks. From thirty-five to fifty-five, a woman needs personality. From fifty-five on, the lady needs cash.

Kathleen Norris

November 26
Why can't life's problems hit us when we're 17 and know everything?

A. C. Jolly

November 27
One must be fond of people and trust them if one is not to make a mess of life.

E. M. Forster

November 28
A statesman is a politician who is held upright by equal pressure from all directions.

Eric Johnston

November 29
The difference between a political campaign speech and an appearance is twenty minutes.

Adlai Stevenson

November 30
No man would listen to you talk if he didn't know it was his turn next.

Edgar W. Howe

December 1
When you're a blond, they take your arm to keep you from falling into an open manhole. But when you're a brunette . . . you're just one of the bunch.

Carol Channing

December 2

It is the malady of our age that the young are so busy teaching us that they have no time left to learn.

Eric Hoffer

December 3

We women do talk too much but even then we don't tell half we know.

Nancy, Lady Astor

December 4

I don't go along with all this talk of a generation gap. We're all contemporaries. There's only a difference in memories, that's all.

W. H. Auden

December 5

The best argument is that which seems merely an explanation.

Dale Carnegie

December 6

Cooking is like love. It should be entered into with abandon or not at all.

Harriet Van Horne

December 7

Statistics are like alienists—they will testify for either side.

Fiorello H. LaGuardia

December 8

I'll match my flops with anybody's but I wouldn't have missed 'em. Flops are a part of life's menu and I've never been a girl to miss out on any of the courses.

Rosalind Russell

December 9

Etiquette means behaving yourself a little better than is absolutely essential.

Will Cuppy

December 10

Cold! If the thermometer had been an inch longer we'd all have frozen to death!

Mark Twain

December 11
I have learned that only two things are necessary to keep one's wife happy. First let her think she's having her way. And second let her have it.

Lyndon B. Johnson

December 12
An ideal husband is one who treats his wife like a new car.

Dan Bennett

December 13
This is a do-it-yourself test for paranoia: you know you've got it when you can't think of anything that's your fault.

Robert Hutchins

December 14
An honest man can never surrender an honest doubt.

Walter Malone

December 15
Nothing in nature is more beautiful than one snowflake, but unfortunately they seldom come that way.

Bill Vaughan

December 16
Nobody can be exactly like me. Sometimes even I have trouble doing it.

Tallulah Bankhead

December 17
Whether women are better than men I cannot say—but I can say they are certainly no worse.

Golda Meir

December 18
Pro football is like nuclear warfare. There are no winners, only survivors.

Frank Gifford

December 19
Love is the strongest force the world possesses, and yet it is the humblest imaginable.

Mahatma Gandhi

December 20
The greater the difficulty the more glory in surmounting it. Skillful pilots gain their reputation from storms and tempests.

Epicurus

December 21
Respect is love in plain clothes.

Frankie Byrne

December 22
I like not only to be loved, but to be told I am loved.

George Eliot

December 23
If youth is a fault, one soon gets rid of it.

Johann von Goethe

December 24
Don't worry about the size of your Christmas tree. In the eyes of children they are all 25 feet tall.

Bill Vaughan

December 25
For God so loved the world, that he gave his only begotten Son, that whosoever believeth in him should not perish, but have everlasting life.

John 3:16

December 26
If a man could have half his wishes, he would double his troubles.

Benjamin Franklin

December 27
There is no surprise more magical than the surprise of being loved. It is the finger of God on a man's shoulder.

Charles Morgan

December 28
Censorship, like charity, should begin at home; but unlike charity, it should end there.

Clare Booth Luce

December 29
Everybody is ignorant, only of different subjects.

Will Rogers

December 30
Thinking is like loving and dying. Each of us must do it for himself.

Josiah Royce

December 31
There's night and day, brother, both sweet things; sun, moon, and stars, brother. Life is very sweet.

George Borrow

Selected by Margery Johnson
Set in Souvenir roman and bold
Designed by Manny Drowne